House of Wisdom

30 Days of Morning Light and Inspiration From Proverbs

By Bryan Hudson, Th.B., B.S., M.S.

Copyright ©2014 Bryan Hudson
Indianapolis, Indiana USA

ISBN# 978-1-931425-13-1

PUBLISHED BY

visionBooks & Media

www.VisioncomSolutions.com
www.VisionBooksMedia.com
www.BryanHudson.com

I0190517

The House of Wisdom
CONTENTS

1.	No Excuses	6
2.	The High Cost of Complacency	8
3.	You'll Get What You Chase	10
4.	Why Options and Choices Seem to be Difficult	12
5.	How to Give to God	14
6.	Benefits of Guarding Your Heart and Focusing Forward	16
7.	Raising Hope and Removing Fear	18
8.	Wisdom Has Friends	20
9.	Is Your Cart in Front of Your Horse?	22
10.	Wisdom for the Broken Vineyard	24
11.	Come Into the House of Wisdom	27
12.	Value of Wisdom	29
13.	How to Have Clarity of Thought	31
14.	The Path Principle	32
15.	The Clean Fear of the Lord	34
16.	Facts about Favor	36
17.	Learning to Listen To Wisdom's Words	39
18.	Furniture in a Field	41
19.	In Love With Wisdom	43
20.	Wisdom's Way to Wealth	45
21.	God's Air Traffic Control Tower	47
22.	Jesus: My Wisdom	49
23.	The Life-Changing Power of Instruction	51
24.	Something More Important Than Good Plans	53
25.	Practical Wisdom	55
26.	Planning to Succeed	57
27.	Four Ways to Become Wiser	59
28.	How to Deal With Enemies	61
29.	Scattering Seed to Increase	63
30.	What We See, What God Sees	65
	About the Author	67

Introduction
How to Use *House of Wisdom* 30-Day Devotional

Proverbs 24:3-4, *Through wisdom a house is built, and by understanding it is established; By knowledge the rooms are filled with all precious and pleasant riches.*

Welcome to this "House of Wisdom" devotional based on the book of Proverbs!

The book of Proverbs is a compilation of wise sayings, general truths, fundamental principles, or rules of conduct. The Hebrew word translated "proverb" is also translated "oracle" and "parable." Most proverbs are short, compact statements that express truths about human behavior using contrasts or direct comparisons. Many proverbs describe the consequences of a particular action or character trait. (Read a full summary on the Book of Proverbs here: *http://www.biblestudytools.com/proverbs*)

The opening chapter of Proverbs explains the purpose of this book written mostly by Solomon: *"Their purpose is to teach people wisdom and discipline, to help them understand the insights of the wise. Their purpose is to teach people to live disciplined and successful lives, to help them do what is right, just, and fair. These proverbs will give insight to the simple, knowledge and discernment to the young."* (Prov. 1:2-4 NLT)

In a world that has lost sight of principles and unchanging foundations, Proverbs offers a steady view of life,

structure for living, and a path to life, prosperity and security—like living in a house.

Jesus, through His life and resurrection, has become our
wisdom: 1 Corinthians 1:30 *But because of Him are ye in
Christ Jesus, who from God is made unto us wisdom and righteousness, and sanctification and redemption.*

Christ provides wisdom. We only need to discover how
wisdom works and apply it to our lives. **Let's go into
the "House of Wisdom" designed by God!**

How to use this devotional:

Following each reading and prayer time, do the following
exercises:

1. Respond to Reflection Question.

2. Write down any insights you gain from the scripture
   reading and commentary.

3. Write down any action items or things you need to do
   based on what you have read.

4. Continue your devotional time as the Lord directs
   you.

*NOTE: Scripture readings and commentary from Proverbs are not in
numerical order.*

~ ***Bryan Hudson,*** *Th.B., B.S., M.S.*

DAY 1   No Excuses

Proverbs 1:20, *Wisdom shouts in the streets. She cries out in the public square. 21 She calls to the crowds along the main street, to those gathered in front of the city gate: 22 "How long, you simpletons, will you insist on being simpleminded? How long will you mockers relish your mocking? How long will you fools hate knowledge. 23 Come and listen to my counsel. I'll share my heart with you and make you wise.*

Throughout the Book of Proverbs wisdom is "personified" or given a personality to gain attention. God uses a woman to personify wisdom probably because we are all naturally more attentive to the voice of a woman, such as our mother. A female's voice is also more penetrating than a male's voice. This is the reason a female voice is used in advanced airplanes to alert pilots.

Wisdom from God is always available so there is no excuse for being "simple-minded," which Webster's Dictionary defines as, "Having or showing a lack of good sense or judgment." Your answer, solution, insight and strategy is never far away. You only need to slow down long enough to listen and learn.

Most of the trouble and traps in life actually **count on** people acting without good sense and judgment, as if something essential will be missed. That pressure is opposite to operating in wisdom.

"Come and listen...I'll share my heart..." We are not born with wisdom in our physical DNA. It has to be received as spiritual DNA from Christ. Just as singing talent has to be developed, the wisdom of God is developed through instruction and action. Relationship with God and wise people is the best path for growing in wisdom and understanding.

Reflection Question: What "trap," if any, do you recognize that resulted from a lack of wisdom?

Key insight I gained today:

Today's action item based on insight:

2
DAY

The High Cost of Complacency

Proverbs 1:32-33, *For simpletons turn away from me—to death. Fools are destroyed by their own complacency. But all who listen to me will live in peace, untroubled by fear of harm.*

Proverbs is full of contrasts and comparisons. Sometimes the best way to learn is to read about the consequences of bad choices by others. This is called learning "vicariously," or through the (flesh) lives of others. Making big mistakes and blunders is a very painful way to learn, if people learn at all. In fact, "experience" is not the best teacher. The wisdom of God in Christ is the best teacher.

One of the greatest enemies of progress is complacency. Here's the definition: "A feeling of quiet pleasure or security, often while unaware of some potential danger."

Feelings alone cannot be trusted anymore than looking at bright sunshine through a window. Conditions outside the window may actually be dangerous, such as a bitter cold day. Complacency can be as self-destructive as drug abuse and smoking cigarettes. Ignoring wisdom while embracing foolishness is a recipe for decline.

On the positive and proactive side, listening to wisdom and instruction come with a guarantee of ultimately living in peace and freedom from the fear of bad outcomes.

Who do you listen to?

Reflection Question: What area(s) of complacency can you displace now through acting with wisdom?

Key insight I gained today:

Today's action item based on insight:

DAY 3 ⋮ You'll Get What You Chase

Proverbs 2:2, *Tune your ears to wisdom, and concentrate on understanding. 3 Cry out for insight, and ask for understanding. 4 Search for them as you would for silver; seek them like hidden treasures. 5 Then you will understand what it means to fear the Lord, and you will gain knowledge of God.*

In the realm of education (in which I earned a Masters of Science degree), we know there is both *active* and *passive* learning. Passive learning is like watching television or listening to someone talk, with no engagement by the learner. Active learning engages the physical senses of the learner and uses something called "authentic context," which provides instruction that relates to the context of the learner's world.

The Spirit of God who inspired Solomon to write this part of Proverbs knows all about learning. This is why he used language that related to the context of the readers. Searching "as you would for silver" or "hidden treasures" is more compelling than just "searching."

On another level, gaining wisdom and understanding is actually **more valuable** to your life than owning silver and earthly treasures. It is ironic that in our world and culture, making money is considered by many to be the greatest objective in life and spiritual matters do not rate very high. When Jesus said that no one can serve two masters (Matt. 6:24), He was talking about God and money/earthly possessions. Material gain and wisdom are not mutually exclusive, but they must not be equally valued.

The greater point to the text is this: What is your level of intensity and desire for God's wisdom and understanding? The writer is saying that when people pursue wisdom and understanding with the same motivation they pursue money and things, they will understand the fear of God and gain divine knowledge. It is a matter of desire and priority.

Reflection Question: What do you pursue more than wisdom and understanding from God? How can you correct that imbalance?

Key insight I gained today:

Today's action item based on insight:

4 Why Options and Choices Seem to be Difficult

Proverbs 2:10, *For wisdom will enter your heart, and knowledge will fill you with joy. 11 Wise choices will watch over you. Understanding will keep you safe.*

Sometimes people struggle with options and choices. They have difficulty deciding which way to go. This is especially true when options and choices appear to be mostly good. We've heard the saying, "Everything that seems good is not necessarily good for you." What people consider "good" is usually driven by what friends and popular culture embrace. If everyone were driving a white car, then a white car would seem to be the good option.

Because God's wisdom and understanding are "holy," these are not subject to the whims of people or popular culture. The best definition of the word "holy" is "other than." The Father, Son, and Holy Spirit is the ultimate being (one God) existing as "Other Than" – absolutely nothing and no one can compare. Believers in Christ are called a "holy nation" (1 Peter 2:9).

As partakers of holy wisdom and understanding from God, options and choices are narrowed by excluding everything that motivates people who lack wisdom, understanding, and divine purpose. When we operate on God's resources, we experience true joy. Within that domain, you can only take the best option and make the correct choice.

Reflection Question: Which options or choices would be easier if you excluded every prideful, worldly, or marketing influence?

Key insight I gained today:

Today's action item based on insight:

5 How to Give to God

Proverbs 3:9, *Honor the Lord with your wealth and with the best part of everything you produce. 10 Then he will fill your barns with grain, and your vats will overflow with good wine.*

This is one of our favorite Scriptures to motivate people to give money to the Lord through our ministries and local churches. It is appropriate for that purpose, but there is much more to it.

It is actually a Scripture that addresses the **quality** of our giving that leads to the quality of our harvest of blessings. Jesus said it this way, *"Give, and it will be given to you. A good measure, pressed down, shaken together and running over, will be poured into your lap. For with the measure you use, it will be measured to you."* (Luke 6:38)

These Scriptures seem to focus only on the amount given, but the quality of giving is more important than the amount. For example, if a person is complaining while giving a large amount, it is neither the "best part" nor a "good measure." While the church that receives the offering will certainly be glad to receive it, the giver may not receive much of a return. In other words, that unwilling giver might receive "wine" (some provision), but not receive "good wine" (maximum or strategic provision).

A person who cannot give a large amount of money (or some other kind of offering), yet offers their "best part" and "good measure" taps into the resources of God's kingdom and grace in a special way.

For example, the best part of our financial offering comes **before** paying taxes and bills. Giving to God what is left over **after** taxes and bills is far from the best part. This way of giving to God cannot be easily explained, but it is easily proven by those who practice it!

The key words in this text are "Honor the Lord." The word **honor** literally means "a valuing." The picture is one of something valuable, precious or weighty, such as gold. Other definitions include: appreciation, esteem, favorable regard, respect.

Much more than what you give to the Lord is the value, esteem, respect, you have towards God when giving it. Anyone you honor will notice it. God does not need honor from us, but because He is honorable, you can only receive blessing from giving Him your "best part" and "good measure." God takes note of being honored.

Reflection Question: What are 1-2 examples of your "best part" that should be given to God?

Key insight I gained today:

Today's action item based on insight:

Benefits of Guarding Your Heart and Focusing Forward

Day 6

Proverbs 4:18 *The way of the righteous is like the first gleam of dawn, which shines ever brighter until the full light of day. 19 But the way of the wicked is like total darkness. They have no idea what they are stumbling over…23 Guard your heart above all else, for it determines the course of your life…25 Look straight ahead, and fix your eyes on what lies before you. 26 Mark out a straight path for your feet; stay on the safe path. 27 Don't get sidetracked; keep your feet from following evil.*

Everything in your life follows the condition of your heart. Emotions, thoughts, and decisions all flow from the heart. People who are sad and bitter consistently make bad decisions because "painful disappointment" (which is the definition of *bitterness*) shapes their thoughts. People who are confused often think others are confused, but its nothing more than distorted perception resulting from their own confusion. When dealing with negative people, remember these words; "Your perception is not my reality."

On the positive side, a heart that is guarded by the grace of God empowers people and produces the following benefits:

1. A bright path, which "feels" like optimism and positive outlook about self and others

2. A brighter path day by day, setbacks not withstanding

3. A clearer course for your life going forward

4. A straight, stable path or foundation

5. Ability to stay your course and not get sidetracked or distracted

Reflection Question: Regarding your heart, what "course correction" do you need to make?

Key insight I gained today:

Today's action item based on insight:

7 Raising Hope and Removing Fear

Proverbs 10:24, *The fears of the wicked will be fulfilled; the hopes of the godly will be granted.*

Fear and hope are strangely related. A lot of the negative things that happen to people are often attributed to fate, to the devil, to other people, and even to God.

While there is certainly no such thing as "mind over matter," there is the reality of "mind over self."

Hopes and fears move us to action both extrinsically (outward) and intrinsically (inward). Hope and fear also motivate us consciously and unconsciously.

Hope and fear are related because both are based in expectation. Hope **expects** a good outcome. Fear **expects** danger and harm. People who live in fear will take unusual measures to guard against imagined threats and dangers. People who have hope will take measures to secure their dreams and bring to pass what they see in their hearts and minds.

Our Scripture text refers to the fears of the "wicked." Is it possible for the godly to have fear? The answer is yes, and the godly won't experience better outcomes if operating in fear.

We should only focus on the hopes that God wants to grant to the godly. So trust Him and live a godly life through Christ.

Reflection Question: What are 1-3 hopes you expect to be granted?

Key insight I gained today:

Today's action item based on insight:

8 Wisdom Has Friends

Proverbs 8:12, *"I, Wisdom, live together with good judgment. I know where to discover knowledge and discernment. 13 All who fear the Lord will hate evil. Therefore, I hate pride and arrogance, corruption and perverse speech. 14 Common sense and success belong to me. Insight and strength are mine. 15 Because of me, kings reign, and rulers make just decrees. 16 Rulers lead with my help, and nobles make righteous judgments. 17 I love all who love me. Those who search will surely find me. 18 I have riches and honor, as well as enduring wealth and justice. 19 My gifts are better than gold, even the purest gold, my wages better than sterling silver! 20 I walk in righteousness, in paths of justice. 21 Those who love me inherit wealth. I will fill their treasuries."*

Wisdom is not a singular virtue. Like a bountiful garden, the wisdom of God is filled with many virtues and benefits. Wisdom has many excellent "friends."

Here, as in many other passages in Proverbs, wisdom is personified. Wisdom is speaking directly to the reader and clearly defining her assets. Giving wisdom a personality is God's way of making the message both powerful and personal. Here's a listing of wisdom's friends from this passage:

1. Good judgment: Everyone has judgment. What is needed is "good" judgment.

2. Knowledge & discernment
3. Common sense
4. Success
5. Insight
6. Strength
7. Leadership ability
8. Riches
9. Enduring wealth
10. Honor
11. Justice
12. Wages (Paydays!)

Reflection Question: Which five "friends" of wisdom do you need now?

Key insight I gained today:

Today's action item based on insight:

9 Is Your Cart in Front of Your Horse?

DAY

Proverbs 24:27, *Do your planning and prepare your fields before building your house.*

Ambition is a powerful emotion and motivator. Ambition defined: *An earnest desire for some type of achievement or distinction, as power, honor, fame, or wealth, and the willingness to strive for its attainment.*

Wanting to build and live in a very nice house is an ambition. It is something to dream about and tell others. We all have ambitions, but ambition without purpose and godly vision can only lead to arrogance.

We use phrases like "putting the cart before the horse" or "major on majors" to express something similar to our Scripture text.

I remember asking God about some property I considered buying. It was as if God said to me, "What about it?" I wanted God to give me a "yea" or "nay" on buying it. He wanted me to do what Proverbs 24:27 said, "plan and prepare." Ultimately, raw ambition is little more than a form of dreamy laziness. Former Federal Reserve Chairman Alan Greenspan once used the phrase, "Irrational exuberance" to describe unrealistic investor attitudes.

Allow hope to sketch an outline of where you want to go, but spend your time planning, preparing, and exercising wisdom.

Reflection Question: What is something you feel ambitious about that needs better planning to make happen?

Key insight I gained today:

Today's action item based on insight:

10 Wisdom for the Broken Vineyard

Proverbs 24:30, *I walked by the field of a lazy person, the vineyard of one with no common sense. 31 I saw that it was overgrown with nettles. It was covered with weeds, and its walls were broken down. 32 Then, as I looked and thought about it, I learned this lesson: 33 A little extra sleep, a little more slumber, a little folding of the hands to rest— 34 then poverty will pounce on you like a bandit; scarcity will attack you like an armed robber.*

If we needed motivation to push aside any temptation to allow laziness or neglect to seep into our lives, this Scripture should drive it out! There is something to be said for neatness, order, and maintaining things that we own.

A lot of what goes wrong in life, including some forms of poverty, has nothing to do with circumstances out of our control. It is interesting that the writer used a vineyard (a grapevine farm) as an example. Jesus used a vineyard for his teaching in John 15:1 *"I am the true grapevine, and my Father is the gardener."*

The Proverb's writer could not have chosen a more difficult plant to use for an object lesson. Vines and vineyards are very difficult to grow and manage. Vines will naturally grow all over the ground, up the sides of walls, around the trunks of trees, and become entirely unmanageable. **Grapevines must be managed** by a vinedresser to guide and provide structure for the vine.

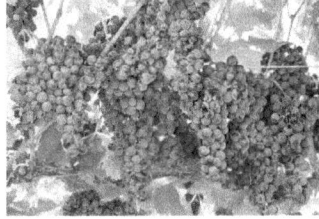

Our lives are more like vineyards than evergreen trees, which require very little maintenance. The bad condition of the vineyard described in our Scripture text was not years in the making. Given the aggressive growth patterns of grapevines, and of our lives, chaos can follow after a only few months of neglect.

Wisdom operates through diligence, maintenance, and a plan for improvement.

Reflection Question: Is there anything broken, or out of order, in your life that diligence could change in a matter of weeks?

Key insight I gained today:

Today's action item based on insight:

11 : Come Into the House of Wisdom

Proverbs 9:1, *Wisdom has built her house; she has carved its seven columns. 2 She has prepared a great banquet, mixed the wines, and set the table. 3 She has sent her servants to invite everyone to come. She calls out from the heights overlooking the city. 4 "Come in with me," she urges the simple. To those who lack good judgment, she says, 5 "Come, eat my food, and drink the wine I have mixed. 6 Leave your simple ways behind, and begin to live; learn to use good judgment."*

Wisdom has a house. Learn how to live in it.

When we abide outside the House of Wisdom, we can find ourselves being easily persuaded and enticed by people, places and powers that see our vulnerability. Wisdom provides a unique perspective on circumstances and people. Without wisdom's perspective, we do not fully see what we are dealing with. God's house of wisdom is also designed to help those "who lack *good* judgment." Everyone has judgment. We look at things and form an opinion. The problem is that our judgment is only as good as our level of wisdom, understanding, and knowledge.

Outside the House of Wisdom, things that are bad for you might actually look good. Outside the house of wisdom, we are mostly impressed by the first, shiniest, loudest, person or thing we see. A lot of failed marriages, bad relationships, and unhealthy entanglements, began as meetings, "romantic" dates or even promiscuous activity outside the House of Wisdom.

There's always room in the House of Wisdom. **Come on in!**

Proverbs 9:6 *"Leave your simple ways behind, and begin to live; learn to use good judgment."*

Reflection Question: What decision(s) made outside the House of Wisdom can you now correct?

Key insight I gained today:

Today's action item based on insight:

12 The Value of Wisdom

Proverbs 9:7 *Anyone who rebukes a mocker will get an insult in return. Anyone who corrects the wicked will get hurt. 8 So don't bother correcting mockers; they will only hate you. But correct the wise, and they will love you. 9 Instruct the wise, and they will be even wiser. Teach the righteous, and they will learn even more. Fear of the Lord is the foundation of wisdom. Knowledge of the Holy One results in good judgment. 11 Wisdom will multiply your days and add years to your life. 12 If you become wise, you will be the one to benefit. If you scorn wisdom, you will be the one to suffer.*

Wisdom and understanding are most appreciated by those who embrace it. People who mock the things of God will likely not accept correction. Such persons need prayer and the saving message of the Gospel of Christ. We would like to think that we can help or "cure" anyone. But the fact remains that the Holy Spirit must help a person become receptive—something the Lord is quite expert at doing!

Wisdom is a virtue best shared among believers in Christ. The "righteous" are people who will honor God and rejoice in His ways. According to Ephesians 4:15-16, the body of Christ "edifies itself" in love. That is, we build each other up, not for selfish reasons, but to become more effective as a community and in reaching our generation for the Kingdom of God.

Verse nine says, *"Fear of the Lord is the foundation of wisdom."* Foundations are vitally important to buildings, especially tall ones. Laying a good foundation is the beginning to any successful building project. The "building project"of our lives requires understanding and living out the principle of the fear of the Lord. I define the fear of the Lord as "A deep desire to please and never displease the Lord."

Upon the firm foundation of godly fear comes "good judgment" (to make wise decisions and choices), long life, and other benefits as God's purpose for our lives may determine.

Reflection Question: In what way(s) can you honor God and value His wisdom?

Key insight I gained today:

Today's action item based on insight:

DAY 13 How to Have Clarity of Thought

Proverbs 16:3 *Commit your works to the Lord, And your thoughts will be established.*

Clarity of thought follows committing your works and plans to the Lord. Good works bring good thoughts, because you were created by God to do good works. (Ephesians 2:10)

When we commit to Him, God takes responsibility for our success!

Sometimes, being unclear in your thinking is an indication that you are on the wrong track or have not fully committed your work to the Lord.

Reflection Question: What prevents you from making a full commitment to God?

Key insight I gained today:

Today's action item based on insight:

14   The Path Principle

Proverbs 7:6, *While I was at the window of my house, looking through the curtain, 7 I saw some naive young men, and one in particular who lacked common sense. 8 He was crossing the street near the house of an immoral woman, strolling down the path by her house...21 So she seduced him with her pretty speech and enticed him with her flattery. 22 He followed her at once, like an ox going to the slaughter. He was like a stag caught in a trap, 23 awaiting the arrow that would pierce its heart. He was like a bird flying into a snare, little knowing it would cost him his life.*

Solomon used various methods to communicate the same message of gaining understanding and wisdom. Chapter Seven uses a first person narrative to describe someone he saw out of his window. He says, *"I saw some naive young men, and one in particular who lacked common sense."*

What made this young man naive? The definition of naive is, "showing a lack of experience, wisdom, or judgment." He also lacked common sense. Why did Solomon regard this young man in this manner? This young man was walking down a path that led past the dwelling of a well known immoral woman. This is called "The Path Principle," a term I first read in a book by Pastor Andy Stanley.

Your path determines your destination. Your intentions and wishes do not determine your destination more than the path that has been chosen. The young man in the story did not know his day would end in sin and destruction because he was seemingly unaware of where his path led.

The message of the story is to recognize the necessity of choosing our paths well. For example, hanging out with people who are up to no good is not just "hanging out," it's a path! Spending time studying the Bible is not just reading. It's a path. Again, since every path has a destination, experiencing prosperity God's way begins with understanding our activities as paths leading to good or bad outcomes.

Reflection Question: What "good intentions" have your mistaken for a good path? What path (s) are you actually on?

Key insight I gained today:

Today's action item based on insight:

15 : The Clean Fear of the Lord

Proverbs 24:21, *Fear the LORD and the king, my son, and do not join with the rebellious, 22 for those two will send sudden destruction upon them, and who knows what calamities they can bring?*

In a world filled with rebellion, respecting and responding properly to higher authority opens the door to greater personal authority. Rebellion is defined as: *Resistance to or defiance of authority, control, or tradition.*

Proverbs 9:10, (NLT) *Fear of the LORD is the foundation of wisdom. Knowledge of the Holy One results in good judgment.*

There is "good" fear and "bad" fear. Bad fear is feeling a sense of terror or doom. This kind of fear is expectation of danger and harm. Most fears are imagined, but some are real. The only good thing about bad fear is that you are motivated to take action to avoid danger. Driving in snow and ice produces a healthy kind of fear that keeps you alert and cautious.

On the other hand, the fear of the Lord is "good." David said in Psalms 19:9, *"The fear of the Lord is clean, enduring forever."*

Good fear is a dread of displeasing the Lord. It is a mindset that says, "I want to please God and not allow my actions to bring Him displeasure." Honor and godly fear are foundational to living a victorious life. Authority flows in a line, or what the military calls a "chain of command."

Those who function in the fear of God place a high value on having a right relationship with God and people with whom they relate. They are "clean" or "pure," not only because foul things are removed. They are clean/pure because it has already been decided.

Reflection Question: How is the "clean" fear of the Lord helping to change your life and please God?

Key insight I gained today:

Today's action item based on insight:

16 Facts about Favor

Proverbs 3:3, *Let love and faithfulness never leave you; bind them around your neck, write them on the tablet of your heart. Then you will win favor and a good name in the sight of God and man.*

A lot has been said and written about the favor of God. Everyone wants favor, which really amounts to help, opportunity, or preferential treatment from God and people. As much as we may talk about self-reliance, the fact remains that we all want help and special treatment.

Divine favor, or favor from God, happens in very unusual ways. Favor can be "supernatural" in your life, because your circumstances require it. Not everyone is well "connected." **Natural favor** comes by associating with the "right" people. In some instances, if you are blessed with good looks and the right body type, this will help attract natural favor.

According to Proverbs 3:3, we can find **supernatural favor** with both God and man by two means; love and faithfulness.

God is love. Jesus gave his life because of God's love for us. People make great sacrifices for others because of love. Love is the greatest and most trustworthy motivator. When you walk in the God kind of love, you abide in a special place of God's power and presence. Not only is love a motivator for positive action, it is also a great power of attraction. Love attracts favor.

Faithfulness attracts favor. In a world of absent commitment and shaky fidelity, faithfulness stands out like a mountain on the horizon.

One year, we vacationed in the Seattle-Tacoma area of Washington. For me, the most amazing sight was Mount Rainier standing tall at 14,400 feet. It was visible from almost any part of both cities. Coming from Indianapolis, which is essentially flat, the sight of that mountain was inspiring and reassuring.

Faithfulness is like Mount Rainier. You can't miss it or ignore it. You can't imagine a landscape without it. You look for it when needing direction.

When love and faithfulness are bound within our hearts, we attract supernatural favor from God and man. You won't have to play mind games, ride somebody's coattails, or be apprehensive. Walking in love and faithfulness through Christ is enough.

Reflection Question: What are 1-2 areas where God has helped you to be faithful?

Key insight I gained today:

Today's action item based on insight:

17 Learning to Listen To Wisdom's Words

Proverbs 4:10 (NLT), *My child, listen to me and do as I say, and you will have a long, good life. 11 I will teach you wisdom's ways and lead you in straight paths. 12 When you walk, you won't be held back; when you run, you won't stumble. 13 Take hold of my instructions; don't let them go. Guard them, for they are the key to life.*

Listening to wisdom is the key to success and safety. We learn through listening. We become skillful through listening, following instructions, and gaining expertise through practice.

As a college instructor, I re-discovered the truth that students whom people consider to be "smart" are mostly very committed listeners and followers of instruction. The habit of listening closely, as to be able to accurately represent what was said, is a talent for some, but something everyone can learn.

The wisdom listeners' promise of living a "long, good life" is not only a spiritual promise, but a practical reality. The simple, wise admonition of "buckle your seat belt" has saved many lives in auto accidents. Ignoring that practical wisdom has also, sadly, resulted in injury and loss of life.

Wisdom is not simply listening to good suggestions. Living in the House of Wisdom is about enriching and saving our own lives, and the lives of others. We all know that life is full of obstacles. To these challenges, wisdom says, *"When you walk, you won't be held back; when you run, you won't stumble."*

We overcome obstacles, not because we had a wisdom "pep talk." We overcome because wisdom provides the understanding, knowledge, and skill to rise above those obstacles through the grace of God through Christ.

When we take God's wisdom seriously, Verse 13 takes on a new weight and meaning, *"Take hold of my instructions; don't let them go. Guard them, for they are the key to life."*

Reflection Question: What is God's wisdom speaking to you right now?

Key insight I gained today:

Today's action item based on insight:

18 Furniture in a Field

Proverbs 24:3, *By wisdom a house is built, and through understanding it is established; 4 through knowledge its rooms are filled with rare and beautiful treasures.*

It has often been said that "Knowledge is Power." According to Proverbs, knowledge can fill "rooms" with many wonderful things, which may be desirable. But knowledge alone is not enough.

Can you imagine a room full of things without a house? How useful would it be to arrange furniture on an empty lot? Knowledge without wisdom and understanding looks like furniture in a field, without a structure or purpose.

Wisdom is the ability to know what to do and where and when to take action. Understanding is knowing the meaning of things. Knowing the "what, where and why" of life **must** come before simply acquiring material possessions.

Therefore, **power** is really found in possessing wisdom and understanding!

As always, the Word of God teaches us the best way to live!

Reflection Question: What do you understand after reading the Scripture and this lesson that you did not know before reading it.

Key insight I gained today:

Today's action item based on insight:

19 In Love With Wisdom

Proverbs 8:17 *I love those who love me, and those who seek me find me*

Love from God is **unconditional**. However, wisdom is **conditional**.

The Bible says that we love God because he first loved us. Here, the text says that wisdom will love those who love wisdom.

God's love for us is based on His mercy towards humanity. God's wisdom requires our involvement and responsibility.

Wisdom is conditional because it is not essential for salvation. This is the nature of God's unconditional love and saving grace. However, for people who have already trusted Christ as Savior, God calls them to **responsibility and wise action**. As James said, *"Faith without works is dead being alone."*

An essential part of maturity in God is accepting responsibility and allowing his grace to lead us to **love the things of God** and to seek those virtues early and diligently.

Reflection Question: What are 1-3 items that you should take responsibility for right now?

Key insight I gained today:

Today's action item based on insight:

20 Wisdom's Way to Wealth

Proverbs 8:12 (NLT), *I, Wisdom, live together with good judgment. I know where to discover knowledge and discernment. 13 All who fear the Lord will hate evil. Therefore, I hate pride and arrogance, corruption and perverse speech. 14 Common sense and success belong to me. Insight and strength are mine. 15 Because of me, kings reign, and rulers make just decrees. 16 Rulers lead with my help, and nobles make righteous judgments. 17 I love all who love me. Those who search will surely find me. 18 I have riches and honor, as well as enduring wealth and justice. 19 My gifts are better than gold, even the purest gold, my wages better than sterling silver! 20 I walk in righteousness, in paths of justice. 21 Those who love me inherit wealth. I will fill their treasuries.*

There is a "right" way to approach the subject of wealth and material blessings. Through wisdom, we can understand how to walk in God's blessings while maintaining a godly and humble attitude. For believers in Christ, material success is a by-product of living according to God's word. Putting first things first is one of the themes of the Book of Proverbs.

Discussions and teachings that focus solely on money, without regard for greater principles, miss the mark of God's agenda. This approach leads to foolishness. It's very convenient to latch onto scriptures that promise benefits, while ignoring scriptures that call us to responsibility in Christ. If we focus on biblical responsibility, the benefits will follow.

Proverbs 8:35-36 confirms the importance of following God's wisdom: *"For whoever finds me finds life and receives favor from the Lord. But those who miss me injure themselves. All who hate me love death."*

Reflection Question: What part of Proverbs 8:12-21 needs your attention right now?

Key insight I gained today:

Today's action item based on insight:

21 God's Air Traffic Control Tower

Proverbs 29:18, (NIV) *Where there is no revelation [vision], people cast off restraint; but blessed is the one who heeds wisdom's instruction.*

We would never consider running through a forest at night. We would not think of servicing the wiring in our electrical panel without knowing how it works. We would not buy a car or a house without carefully considering costs and budgets. **What we will do** sometimes is make a major decision without praying and consulting the word and wisdom of God.

These four statements describe the importance of "revelation" or vision. The *New Living Translation* uses the phrase, "divine guidance." Understanding and insight are obviously very important. When you see chaos, confusion, and broken lives, this is usually evidence that "restraint" has been cast off. Not many people, especially children and youth, can restrain themselves from foolish and bad behaviors if there is no guiding influence. No one is born with revelation, vision, or divine guidance. It's like education—everyone needs it.

One year, we had our church parking lot seal-coated, but the contractor was not able to paint the parking stripes before Sunday service. On Sunday morning, people parked their cars in strange ways, even those who had been parking on the same lot for years! The absence of lines contributed to a lack of restraint, not because of any kind of rebellion, just a lack of structure.

God's wisdom provides "lines" and a framework for our lives. None of this is designed by God to restrict us. In reality, we are empowered to reach our full potential by being distraction-free. It is comparable to how the airport regulates when/where airplanes take off and land. Pilots don't shout at controllers in the Control Tower, "Hey, I want to take off NOW on that runway over there!" Everyone's safety and efficient travel is ensured when pilots follow the instructions of the Control Tower.

God wants to help us in the same way through wisdom and instruction.

***

Reflection Question: What are 2-3 distractions you can clear to prepare your life for "take off?"

Key insight I gained today:

Today's action item based on insight:

The House of Wisdom

22 Jesus: My Wisdom

1 Corinthians 1:30 *But of Him you are in Christ Jesus, who became for us wisdom from God—and righteousness and sanctification and redemption.*

NOTE: This lesson in "House of Wisdom" is not based in the Book of Proverbs.

There are many benefits that come with the New Birth and union with Christ. This Christian life is much more than going to church, not going to hell, and going to heaven.

We received grace to possess virtues and blessings that would be impossible to gain by any other means. Along with the new nature we received comes a kind of spiritual "DNA." Science summarizes human DNA as, *"the fundamental and distinctive characteristics or qualities of someone."* That's a good description of what we have in Christ!

Our Scripture text identifies the following characteristics of our spiritual nature from Jesus Christ:

1. **Wisdom**: Ability to make good choices and use understanding and knowledge

2. **Righteousness**: Right standing with God

3. **Sanctification**: Set apart to God for holy and high purpose

4. **Redemption**: Purchased by Jesus' life and blood. Free from all claims of sin.

These are not virtues that we seek. These are virtues that we possess because of Christ. Just as talented people have to be coached and developed over many years, believers in Christ need to "grow in grace."

Reflection Question: Write one statement describing your spiritual DNA, "Through Christ I have_____"

Key insight I gained today:

Today's action item based on insight:

DAY 23: The Life-Changing Power of Instruction

Proverbs 15:32 *He who disdains instruction despises his own soul, But he who heeds rebuke gets understanding.*

Receiving God's best and giving God our best begins with an assignment. It is fully realized by recognizing the importance of instruction. Instruction and assignments are provided for our protection and provision.

Think of all the best things in your life. Now think of the broken or unfulfilled things in your life. A lot of disappointment in your life is related to instructions you ignored or did not take seriously. A wise person once said, *"If I can help you change how you respond to an instruction, I can help you change your life."*

Imagine driving on a long trip on a highway without signs or directions. That would essentially be a trip to "nowhere." The fact that we need instruction confirms our need to learn and gain wisdom along with understanding. We also need people in our lives who know more than we know. This is especially true in knowing God and His Word.

It is not only a matter of receiving instruction, but of being better at responding to instructors and their instructions.

Prov. 6:23 *For the commandment is a lamp, And the law a light; Reproofs of instruction are the way of life*

Reflection Question: What are 1-2 instructions you received in the past six months that need follow-up or action taken?

Key insight I gained today:

Today's action item based on insight:

24 Something More Important Than Good Plans

Proverbs 16:3 *Commit to the LORD whatever you do, and your plans will succeed.*

Sometimes I hear this comment: "When God tells me what to do, I'll do it." I find that people operating on this mindset end up waiting for a very, very long time for God to tell them what to do. As a matter of fact, they may still be waiting!

It is not that God does not speak to his people or lead and guide them. It's more a matter of how God wants to work in our lives. We tend to focus on our current feelings, pressing needs, and churning ambitions. God sees much more. He knows the state of our hearts and sees further ahead in order to prepare us for the future. We need to keep our hearts clear and committed to the Lord.

When Samuel went looking for a replacement for King Saul, who was neither committed to the Lord nor obedient, he was impressed by the sight of Eliab, one of David's brothers. However, God spoke to Samuel, *"Do not consider his appearance or his height, for I have rejected him. The LORD does not look at the things man looks at. Man looks at the outward appearance, but the LORD looks at the heart."* (1 Samuel 16:7)

Eliab looked the part, but God saw his heart and said, "Not this one." The person everyone overlooked was David, because of his lowly status as a shepherd and his small stature.

Successful plans begin with a fully committed heart. Committed not first to succeeding, but to living in the grace, wisdom, and character of Christ. Certainly, people can succeed in life without God, but this approach can only amount to "gaining the world" and "losing one's soul." (Matthew 16:26)

Reflection Question: In what ways do you need to commit to God today?

Key insight I gained today:

Today's action item based on insight:

25 Practical Wisdom to Stay on Your Pathway of Life

Proverbs 10:17, *People who accept discipline are on the pathway to life, but those who ignore correction will go astray.*

The book of Proverbs often refers to a preferred pathway. In this text it refers to "the pathway of life."

In our language there is a word called "pragmatic." Being pragmatic is about looking at the practical consequences of actions before actions are taken. The person who is pragmatic first considers what is best and then builds a plan to achieve it. For example, if being out of debt is the best objective, a pragmatist will not use a credit card for consumer debt.

A person on the path of life is someone who does not have a problem accepting correction from God and wise people. Sometimes people are so concerned about hurt feelings that they refuse to give or receive correction. Don't let your emotions get in the way of receiving what you need to stay on the path of life. Whatever consequences or emotions that may follow correction cannot be worse than straying off a good pathway.

Reflection Question: What practical discipline should you apply to your life now to avoid a future problem?

Key insight I gained today:

Today's action item based on insight:

26 Planning to Succeed

Proverbs 16:1(NLT), *We can make our own plans, but the Lord gives the right answer.*

The old saying is true, "People do not plan to fail, they fail to plan." God will not do our planning for us simply because developing a plan is our responsibility, not His. We have delegated authority from the Lord, but not delegated action. We need God's "answer" to the many options that good planning creates. This is the value of "waiting on the Lord," (Psalm 27:14) which is not waiting for God to do something that is our responsibility.

Proverbs 16:3 *Commit your actions to the Lord, and your plans will succeed.*

After we have consulted with God about our plans, we seek wisdom about next actions. It is not enough to commit to what we've already planned to do. We need to submit those actions to the Lord so that He can perfect them and give us specific wisdom on each item. It is in the committing of action plans to the Lord that we discover grace for success.

Planning is an interactive process that includes the elements of: vision, time, information, financial resources, other people, tools suited to the task, and more. Because there are so many moving parts to a plan, we rely on God's wisdom to sort everything out.

Reflection Question: For which of your action plans, do you need to slow down and fully commit that plan to the Lord?

Key insight I gained today:

Today's action item based on insight:

Four Ways to Become Wiser

Proverbs 13:20, *Walk with the wise and become wise; associate with fools and get in trouble.*

It has been said that a person can be known by the company he keeps. After our relationship with the Lord, our relationships with other people makes the greatest impact on our lives. Walking with the wise should be our objective, but achieving this is not as easy as it sounds.

How can you identify wise people in your life? The first step is to avoid acting foolishly or connecting with foolish people. Foolish means, *"resulting from or showing a lack of sense; ill-considered, unwise, a foolish action, a foolish speech, lacking forethought or caution."*

In a world consumed with darkness and deceit, simply avoiding foolishness is wise. However, spiritual growth and progress don't come only by "not doing," but it is a good place to start. It is better to be "pro-active," which means, *"Tending to initiate change rather than reacting to events."*

Four ways to walk with the wise and become wiser:

1. Listen to, or read books from, people who do productive work and help others improve.

2. Ask good questions of people who are experts. Don't be intimidated by people who know more than you. This is how we all learn.

3. Read the Bible and listen to the Lord. Who's wiser than God?

4. Be prepared to change your mind and change your opinions when better information becomes available.

Reflection Question: Who are 1-3 wise people in your life whom you should listen to more than you do?

Key insight I gained today:

Today's action item based on insight:

28 How to Deal With Enemies

Proverbs 16:7, *When people's lives please the Lord, even their enemies are at peace with them.*

We spend too much time in conflict with people and too little time focused on pleasing God. An "enemy" is something or someone that creates hardship for your progress. It is something or someone that devalues, rather than values you.

Now, before you conjure up the faces and names of people who can be classified as "enemies" remember this Scripture, *"For we do not wrestle against flesh and blood, but against principalities, against powers, against the rulers of the darkness of this age."* (Ephesians 6:12)

We don't overcome enemies by focusing on people and circumstances. God's ways often seem illogical. This is because His power does not rely on our understanding. We should be focused on pleasing the Lord and living victoriously in the spiritual realm, which is the framework for your natural life. For example, if we provide good consistent maintenance for our automobiles, we won't have to think about all the things that could go wrong.

Pleasing God is another way of saying, *"Seek first the Kingdom of God and His righteousness, and all these things will be added to you."* (Matt. 6:33)

When we please God, every enemy is disarmed!

Reflection Question: What can you do now to please God rather than fretting about your enemies?

Key insight I gained today:

Today's action item based on insight:

29 Scattering Seed to Increase

Proverbs 11:24-25, *There is one who scatters, yet increases more; And there is one who withholds more than is right, But it leads to poverty. 25 The generous soul will be made rich, And he who waters will also be watered himself.*

Giving and generosity have always been a part of prospering God's way. This is another action that seems illogical: As we scatter our seed, God causes us to increase. If we withhold too much, it leads to decrease. Giving to the Lord does not cause lack, and failing to give does not help one prosper.

Most everything that relates to living involves the principles or cycles of sowing and reaping.

Genesis 8:22, (NKJV), *While the earth remains, seedtime and harvest, cold and heat, winter and summer, And day and night shall not cease.*

There is a principle working in the earth called *"Seedtime and harvest."* This can be understood as, 1) Seed, 2) Time, 3) Harvest. The Scripture also indicates that life has cycles and seasons. When give of our three "T's" (Time, Treasure, & Talents), its like putting good **seed** into good soil. After a period of **time**, we can expect a **harvest**.

I have witnessed the benefits of this promise for my whole Christian life, over and over again, *".....He who waters will also be watered himself."*

We should not be focused on clinging to what we have (which God gave us) or finding a way to get something from others. We should be more focused on "watering" or nourishing and refreshing others. This habit and lifestyle leads to tremendous blessing at all levels of life.

Reflection Question: What is the status of your giving of Time, Treasure and Talents? Are you giving all three to the Lord?

Key insight I gained today:

Today's action item based on insight:

30 DAY What We See / What God Sees

Proverbs 21:2, *People may be right in their own eyes, but the Lord examines their heart.*

One of the great advantages of knowing the Lord is having the Holy Spirit examine our hearts. Obviously, we only know what we know. We tend to be persuaded only by our own points of view.

We are inherently **subjective**, meaning that we trust our own feelings more than anything else. God helps us to become **objective**, meaning that we can look more independently at our own circumstances and perspectives. Being overly subjective leads to self-deception and stagnation, like a body of water with no fresh source becomes stagnant.

Becoming more objective requires taking in sources that are "bigger" than yourself and challenge your subjective assumptions. These objective sources include: The Bible, your pastor and **authentic** spiritual leaders (not just folk who "act/talk" spiritual), your parents, grandparents, facts, and friends who are not afraid to tell you the truth.

Let the Lord examine your heart, and be willing to change your heart and mind. The word "repent" literally means, "to change one's mind." This is the beginning of transformation and elevation in life.

Reflection Questions: How has being subjective about a situation prevented you from achieving clarity and elevation in life? Being objective, what does God's word say about it?

Key insight I gained today:

Today's action item based on insight:

About the Author

Rev. Bryan Hudson has a multifaceted ministry and professional expertise focused on inspiring and empowering people to know God and achieve the best in their lives. Bryan's training has enabled him to merge ministry with media: Th.B. (Theology), B.S. (Media Arts & Science), M.S. (Education: Instructional Systems Technology).

As a writer, educator, producer, and Bible teacher, Bryan communicates insights on important issues and technologies to deliver solutions to people in need as well as equip leaders to effectively serve their organizations and communities.

He is the founder and senior pastor of *New Covenant Church & Ministries* in Indianapolis, Indiana. Bryan also directs *Vision Communications*, a progressive multimedia firm that creates cutting-edge traditional media and new media. He has conducted summer multimedia training workshops for young men and women to equip and inspire them to use new media in positive ways.

As an instructional designer and former adjunct professor, Bryan Hudson developed and taught a 300-level course at *Crossroads Bible College* in Indianapolis, *New Media for Urban Ministry*.

Bryan is married to Patricia Hudson, a public school educator. They have four grown children and reside in Indianapolis, Indiana.

Twitter: @ChurchMediaGuy
BryanHudson.com
NewCovenant.org
VisionBooksMedia.com

www.ingramcontent.com/pod-product-compliance
Lightning Source LLC
Chambersburg PA
CBHW060040040426
42331CB00032B/1942